Life Around the World
School in Many Cultures

Revised Edition

by Heather Adamson

Consulting Editor: Gail Saunders-Smith, PhD

CAPSTONE PRESS

a capstone imprint

Pebble Plus is published by Capstone Press,
1710 Roe Crest Drive, North Mankato, Minnesota 56003.
www.mycapstone.com

Library of Congress Cataloging-in-Publication Data is available on the Library of Congress website.
ISBN: 978-1-5157-4290-6 (hardback)
ISBN: 978-1-5157-4239-5 (paperback)
ISBN: 978-1-5157-4359-0 (ebook pdf)

Editorial Credits
Sarah L. Schuette, editor; Alison Thiele, set designer; Kara Birr, photo researcher

Photo Credits
Getty Images: Christina Sussman, 19; iStockphoto: davidf, 17, vinhdav, 11; Newscom: ABIR SULTAN/EPA,
7; Shutterstock: De Visu, 5, FredS, 1, Joseph Sohm, 13, Monkey Business Images, cover, Nadejda Ivanova, 15,
Pressmaster, 9, 21

Note to Parents and Teachers

The Life around the World set supports national social studies standards related to culture
and geography. This book describes and illustrates school in many cultures. The
images support early readers in understanding the text. The repetition of words and
phrases helps early readers learn new words. This book also introduces early readers
to subject-specific vocabulary words, which are defined in the Glossary section. Early
readers may need assistance to read some words and to use the Table of Contents,
Glossary, Read More, Internet Sites, and Index sections of the book.

Printed and bound in the USA.
082017   010680R

Table of Contents

Places to Learn

Students go to school
in many cultures.
How is your school
like other schools?

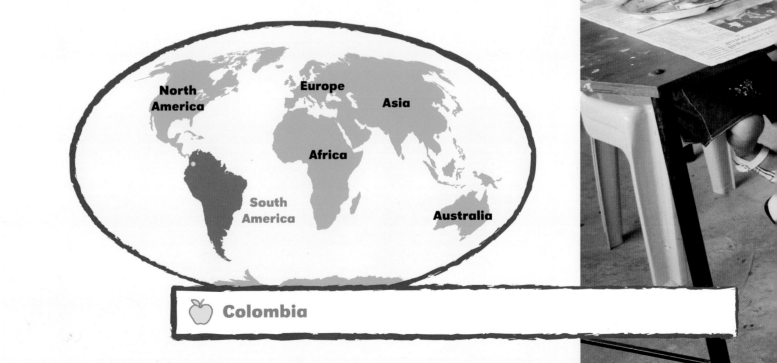

North America

Europe

Asia

Africa

South America

Australia

🍎 Colombia

Teachers work at school.

They teach many subjects.

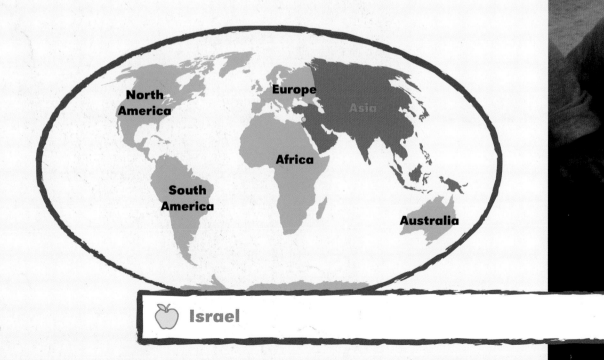

North America

Europe

Asia

South America

Africa

Australia

🍎 Israel

In Class

Students learn in classrooms. A girl in the United States does math on a chalkboard.

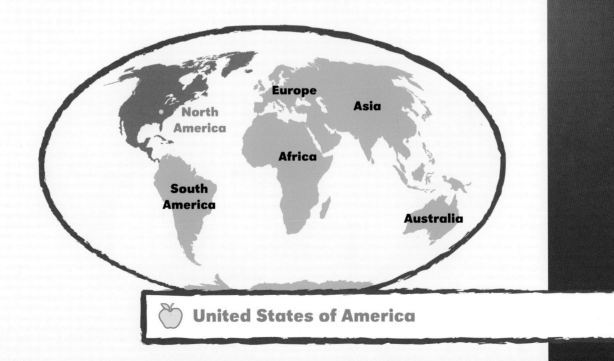

🍎 United States of America

Students learn outside.

A class in Vietnam studies

science and art at a park.

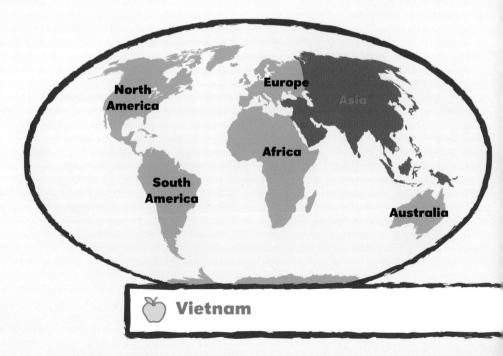

Students take notes.

A boy in Africa

listens to his teacher.

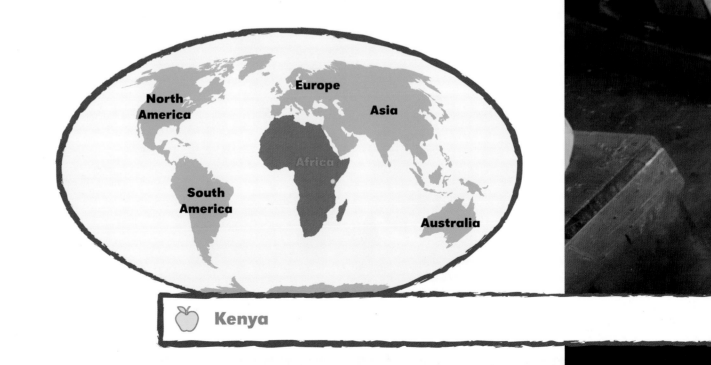

Kenya

Fun at School

Students go on field trips.
A class in France learns
about a castle.

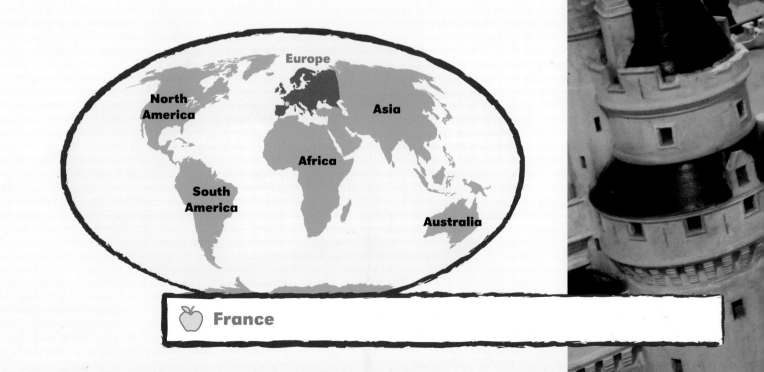

🍎 France

Students take lunch breaks.

Friends in Australia

eat together outside.

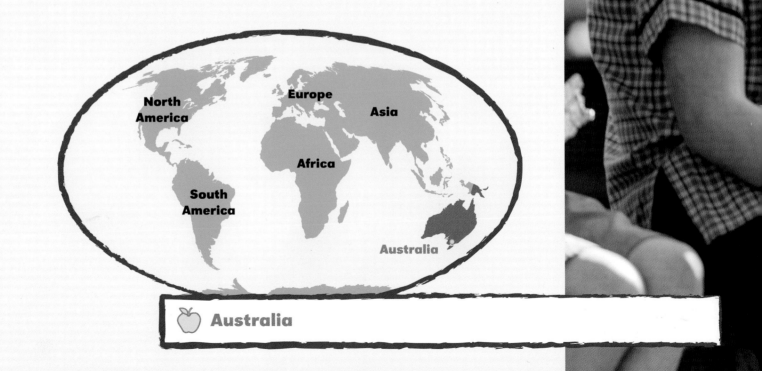

Australia

Students play at recess.

A girl in Africa jumps rope.

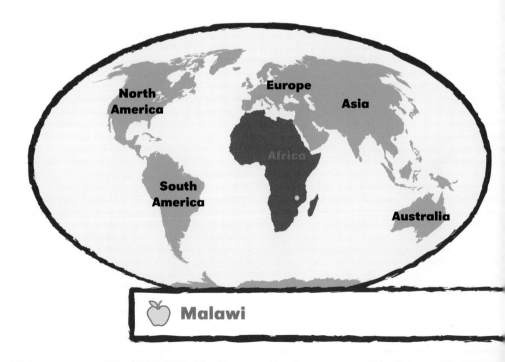

Your School

Around the world, students laugh and learn at school. Where do you go to school?

The Netherlands

Glossary

classroom—a room in a school where classes are taught; classrooms can be in buildings or places outside where students gather.

culture—the way of life, ideas, customs, and traditions of a group of people

field trip—a trip to see and learn something new; classes often go on field trips to museums, zoos, and other interesting places.

math—the study of numbers, shapes, and measurements and how they relate to each other

science—the study of nature and the world

subject—an area of study; students learn subjects such as math, science, art, and music at school.

Read More

Doering, Amanda. *School ABC: An Alphabet Book.* A+ Books: Alphabet Books. Mankato, Minn.: Capstone Press, 2005.

Miller, Jake. *Who's Who in a School Community.* Communities at Work. New York: PowerKids Press, 2005.

Rayner, Amanda. *Going to School.* One World. North Mankato, Minn.: Smart Apple Media, 2006.

Internet Sites

FactHound offers a safe, fun way to find Internet sites related to this book. All of the sites on FactHound have been researched by our staff.

Here's how

1. Visit *www.facthound.com*

2. Choose your grade level.

3. Type in this book ID **1429600217** for age-appropriate sites. You may also browse subjects by clicking on letters, or by clicking on pictures and words.

4. Click on the **Fetch It** button.

FactHound will fetch the best sites for you!

Index

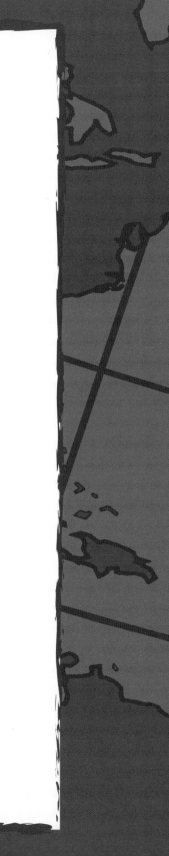

Word Count: 113
Grade: 1
Early-Intervention Level: 12